WONDER WALK

Written by Poppy O'Neill
Illustrated by Diobelle Cerna

Collins

There's beauty all around, if you look carefully. Let's go on a mindful **wonder** walk and see how many fascinating things we can find. Being mindful means slowing down, listening and noticing the world around you. Not only is it interesting, but it also makes your mind and body feel good!

geraniums

What can you spot right outside your home?

You know this place very well, but every day, nature is slowly growing and changing. Pretend it's your first time visiting.

What do you notice?
How many colours can you count?

moss

Look up. Can you see any plants that climb?

They stick to the walls like a spider, with tiny **tendrils**, roots or sticky pads. Nature grows in all directions. Look forwards, backwards, left and right – you'll find there's so much to see.

> What else can you spot high up?

Here is a small patch of nature. Smaller than a park, but not someone's garden – it's like an island of green.

Do you have a place like this nearby?

Take a moment to look closer than you usually do.

What fascinating creatures and plants make this their home? **Venture** into tiny worlds – what new sights, textures and smells will you discover?

Nature isn't always easy to spot, but you'll find it if you try. These plants are **resilient** and **determined**, growing in the cracks. Some people call them weeds because they grow without being planted, but perhaps they're just as beautiful as the flowers we plant on purpose.

Hart's tongue fern

dandelion

How many determined little plants can you spot?

Gardeners plan ahead so that these planters will grow full of flowers. Like a **slow-motion** firework display, they bloom in different shapes of purples, reds and yellows.

Can you spot the patterns?
How do you think a gardener makes designs like that?

Let's visit the playground, there's lots to do here. The birds are **swooping** and singing above the trees.

What game could they be playing?

Their song mixes with the sounds of children playing in the playground.

Under the trees it's quiet and peaceful. Some of the trees have been here for over 100 years, while others are only one or two years old. Light comes softly through the leaves and the wind rustles them gently.

oak

Take deep, mindful breaths.

Can you smell the trees around you? What does the bark feel like against your hand? Spending time with trees helps our bodies and minds feel calm.

beech

Crouch down to look in the pond.
There are plants that **thrive** next to water,
and others that grow up from the bottom
of the pond. Under the murky water it's
like an enchanted world.

iris

Imagine a fish exploring the cool, clear water under the surface.

What treasures would it find?

common great diving beetle

blunt-leaved pondweed

Here the grass is short and neat, and here it's long and wild, like a jungle.

Which is best for running on in bare feet? Which is best for tiny creatures to live in?

crested dog's tail

Anywhere can be full of wonder,
if you take the time to look.

On the way home, there will be something new to notice.

Glossary

determined	to be focused and not give up
Hart's tongue fern	an evergreen plant which often grows in cracks
resilient	the ability to keep going, even when it feels difficult
slow-motion	to play something back at a slower speed
swooping	to move quickly in a smooth path
tendrils	thin stems growing from plants, which curl around other objects for support
thrive	to grow successfully
venture	to explore in a brave way
Virginia creeper	a climbing plant with bright red leaves
wonder	the feeling of amazement caused by something interesting

Index

beech 15
begonia 10
blunt-leaved
   pondweed 17
clematis 19
common great
   diving beetle 17
dandelion 8, 22
geraniums 2
fern 6
Hart's tongue fern 8
iris 16, 22

ivy 5, 23
ladybird 7
moss 3, 23
oak 14, 22
parsley 19, 22
petunia 11
pigeon 13, 23
sparrow 6, 23
starling 13, 22
tulip 10, 22
Virginia Creeper 5
woodlouse 7

 Ideas for reading

Written by Gill Matthews
Primary Literacy Consultant

Reading objectives:
- discuss and clarify the meanings of words, linking new meanings to known vocabulary
- make inferences on the basis of what is being said and done
- answer and ask questions
- participate in discussion about books, poems and other works that are read to them and those that they can read for themselves, taking turns and listening to what others say

Spoken language objectives:
- articulate and justify answers, arguments and opinions
- participate in discussions, presentations, performances, role play, improvisations and debates

Curriculum links: Science: Living things and their habitats
Interest words: mindful, wonder, fascinating, noticing, interesting
Word count: 673
Resources: pictures, paper and pens

Build a context for reading

- Give children 30 seconds to look closely at the front cover of the book and then ask them to turn it face down. Challenge them to name as many things as they can that they saw on the cover.
- Read the title. Explore what children think a wonder walk might be.
- Read the back cover blurb. Ask what they think *mindful* and *wondrous* might mean. If necessary, clarify the meanings of these words.
- Ask children what wondrous things they could see in their neighbourhood or in the area around their school.

Understand and apply reading strategies

- Read pp2–3 aloud, using appropriate expression and intonation.
- Ask children how they feel about being mindful and how they think it would help them.